Love: 365 Happy Meditations

Copyright 2010 Richard Kirsten Daiensai

Published by
Documentary Media
3250 41st Avenue SW
Seattle, WA 98116
(206) 935-9292
books@docbooks.com
www.documentarymedia.com

First Edition, 2010
Printed in China

Text and artwork: Richard Kirsten Daiensai
Book Design: Paul Langland Design
Publisher: Petyr Beck
Editor: Judy Gouldthorpe
Project Manager: Rick Kirsten, the Kirsten Gallery

For inquiries about Richard Kirsten Daiensai, contact:
The Kirsten Gallery
5320 Roosevelt Way NE
Seattle, WA 98105
r2thetop@hotmail.com
www.kirstengallery.com

Library of Congress Cataloging-in-Publication Data
Daiensai, Kirsten, 1920-
Love : 365 happy meditations / Kirsten Daiensai. — 1st ed.
    p. cm.
ISBN 978-1-933245-21-8 (alk. paper)
1. Love—Meditations. I. Title.
BL626.4.D35 2010
204'.32—dc22
2010034518

to BUTA with Love ♥

LOVE

365 Happy Meditations

Richard Kirsten Daiensai

Richard Kirsten Daiensai ♥
2011

Documentary Media
Seattle, Washington

Dedicated to my wife, Elaine

Introduction

Richard C. Kirsten, whose spiritual name as a Zen Buddhist priest is "Daiensai," is known for his paintings, original prints, bronze sculpture, and especially his meditations. *Love: 365 Happy Meditations* is his second in a series of published collections of meditations and art, expanding on his 2004 collection titled *Smile*.

Daiensai's art and writings celebrate the connectedness of heart, mind, and spirit. In this book, he focuses on the vitality of love through meditations as well as 52 images of his original artwork. Much more than an emotion, love for Daiensai is an essential mode of being in the world. His meditations reveal love to be the cornerstone of a happy and fulfilling life. Beyond ecstasy and pain, love, as Daiensai describes it, is the secret to bringing these extremes into balance.

Although Daiensai has numbered the meditations, this is more for reference than to indicate a reading order. While each meditation stands alone as an inspiration in itself, there is often meaningful interplay between several nearby meditations, as well as a circling back to ideas and themes touched upon in other parts of the book. While the number of meditations corresponds to the number of days in the year, this is not meant to symbolize the beginning and ending of a year. Rather, it is meant to evoke a coming full circle, the eternity that unfolds from the cycle of years.

Because of this, there is no wrong way to read the meditations. Daiensai's hope is that you take meaning and fulfillment from them as you find your own path through the book.

*i pray
that every season
of your life
be filled with love
and happiness*

2 *true love*
   keeps no record of wrongs (1 cor 13)

3 be kind and caring and
   love
   will find you

4 *the pine*
has
no voice
but
when the wind
blows
it sings its love

5 i am me
and you are you
but with love
we are one

*₆ what a joy
just to see you
who radiates
love*

7 my life
is full
and complete
because
all love
is within me

8 *in an artist's life*
every color
is an ecstasy
of love

9 words
from the heart
of love
awaken
love in others

10 *just to see your smile
is a celebration of love*

the dew on the grass
is dreaming
of love
briefly

12 *life and love*
are only known
by living them

13 in all humanity
i search for love
and compassion

14   my love
look upon a star
and realize
just how small we are

15   *it is love for the earth*
that would heal the earth

16   love
is something that nobody
likes cold

17 the only path
to inner peace
is love

18 if you love
your rewards
will be fruitful

19 *think*
with your heart
of love
and dwell in the richness
of love

20 my art
and my writing
and deeds
are my way
of making
love
love
love
to everyone

21 a kiss
is no kiss
if there is
no love
in it

22 be happy
all life

some sun some rain
love heals

23 love
people
for what they are
not for what you think they should be

24 love
is the heart
of the universal sacred spirit

25 *when the heart sings love*
the soul sings with it

26 *may a heart overflowing with love*
bring you health
peace and tranquility

O-JIZO-SAN
The Healing
Monk.

2009

DaienSai

"ODE TO LOVE"

DAIENSAI

2008

27 the harmony of love
is the sweetest
soft song

28 an honest smile
carries love
at all times

29 *i was born*
to love
you

30 with a heart
overflowing
with love and gratitude
i thank you for all your kindness

31 *may you be blessed*
    with the understanding
    of unconditional love

32 i send you
    a tsunami of love
    and healing prayers

O-Binzuru The Healer
A/P Linocut – Zuiseni Temple Japan
KIPSTEV – DAISOE 大祖 笑

33 i bring you gratitude
respect
and love
on your birthday
with prayers
of love and healing

34 *may the god of birthdays embrace you*
with love
good health and joy
on this your birthday

35 let all your work
and deeds
be born from love

36 spend your life
seeking wealth
and your heart will be empty
of all that really matters—
love

37 *love illuminates life*

38 the spring breeze comes
and the blossoms
quiver
like
the happy love
in my heart

KIRSTEN   DRENSKI

39 *let the warm winds of love*
caress
your friends
and family

40 live in love and faith
like the flowers
of heaven and earth

41 fill the hearts
of all who you meet
with the comfort of love
and light
and faith

42 from much love
i was born
for love
i live
and in all love and lives
i will return to love

I LOVE YOU
MY ETERNAL LOVE
MY ONLY DESIRE
I ADORE YOU....
MY ECSTACY
JOY
I HONOR YOU
HEART-MIND AND SOUL
MY HEAVEN
大
天

43 *the spirit of love*
opens the flowers of love
within the heart

44 *all the universes in the cosmos know love*

45 together
at the table
for even a snack
love
makes it a festival

46 *oh lord of lords*
increase the light
of love
within me
and all humanity

47 love
is an endless mystery

48 even an old glove
seeks the love and warmth
of fingers

49 a wave of love
can wash away
footprints
of hatred

50 love
is a feast
yet
many are starving

51 let us
with joy
and love
fill our hearts every moment
with love

dear love
every time i think of you
flowers bloom in my heart

"EVERYTIME,
I SEE YOU
FLOWERS BLOOM
IN MY HEART."

53 *we are in love
and dance
on the same flower*

54 the dark side of love is jealousy

55 each
unborn seed
of love
voyages
amongst the stars
patiently
waiting to be reborn

56 *no sense of time*
or place
round or square
up or down
no north
south
east
or west
only the awakening
to the bliss
of love

57 without desire and love
nothing is accomplished

58 the sacred stream
of the spiritual love
its waters clear
lead to divine heart
and mind

59 *love is love*
even if just putting your thoughts
around each other

60 the god
you love
is the god
that touches you
with love

61 growing old is for the birds
or is it
with age our love grows deeper
and stronger

62 *the ecstasy of love*
opens the door
to transformation

63 i love and pay respect
to all my ancestors
who also love me

64 don't wait
to show your love
by kissing a tombstone

65 *hate*
only exists where there is an absence of love

66 please know that your inner heart of love
also teaches others
in all ways
of love

67 *for the unconditional love*
that a pet gives
to us
we give thanks

68 the three virtues
meditate on them—
love
faith
and hope

69 *your heart thoughts*
of love
are seeds that you emanate
to others

70 be happy and love
worry will make you sick

71 *learn to bless everything*
that touches your heart and soul
with love

★KIRSTEN

DAIENSAI天

be happy
while awaiting
love
and happiness

73 *love*
lives
in a smile

DAiENSal

74 have a talk
with
your heart
and know
the depth
of your love

75 *it is the path*
of love
and desire
that takes us on the path
we choose

76 silence and solitude
strengthen
the divine spirit
of love
work and deeds

77 *the buddha nature*
it emanates
love
and healing

78 love
and ecstasy
is sometimes hidden
but always present
no one knows who gave it birth
but
it is older than old
and here
to stay

79 *even before*
the beginning
cosmic love
was everywhere

80 love—
sometimes
the dream chases
reality
sometimes reality
chases the dream
and
dream chases dream
sometimes

81 *sometimes*
love cannot be taught
but the wisdom of love
is passed
from heart to heart

82 make love the sun
in your heart
without love
we grow old
before our time

83 *the healing energy*
    of the heart of love
    is not known
    by most of humanity

84 of course
    this life
    is your life

    now
    but love and respect your ancestors
    in all your lives

85 *may love*
with all
of its very positive energy
be with you all the days
of your life

86 how wonderful
how love
enters
our dreams

87 *even in silence*
my heart speaks of love

88 venerate love
in your every thought
and
non-thought

89 *yes*
sex and sensuality
are an important
part of love
between man and woman

KIRSTEN

DAIENSAI

*every child
is a child of love
hopefully*

91 *love*
can be intoxicating

92 love is an enchantress
embrace her spell
and you will always have a gift
worthy of giving

93   the bed of love
is an altar of love

94   *the brush that had a mind of its own
painted love*

95   some hearts
have
an iron gate
always shut
to love and compassion

the cosmic kiss
the meeting of two souls
in love

she duck
me duck
swimming together as symbol
of marriage and love

98 the compassionate love song
in my heart
can be heard
by all the gods

99 *love is the food of life*
trust in love
and you will be happy

100 let us enjoy
     a festival of love

101 *you*
     my long love
     are far away
     and yet
     our love is forever
     wherever

102 may our life together
     be one of love
     always

103 *kindness and gratitude*
are the path
to love

104 even a mask
can express love

105 love
love
love
love
love
love
is
a wonderful mantra

106　my entire body
is one
with the earth
but
my heart of love
is one
with heaven and earth
and the cosmos

107　*sensual human*
at all times
a sensual joy
of the many
forms of love

love
and dream
by the light
of the midnight moon

109 the juice of love
     is the nectar
     of the cosmos

110 *it is the heart*
     that is the temple of love

111 my life is an oyster of love
     and your love
     is its pearl

112 *to love is to find pleasure*
in the happiness of the person loved

113 let your heart
of love
do the thinking
and feeling
of love

114 the bird of love
sings
even in total
darkness

115 the universe of love
doesn't exist
if you don't know
love

116 *no reason needed*
just smile
laugh
and love

117 the kingdom
of love and light
is within you
awaken to it
and you will be healed

118 the joys of life
exist
for those whose hearts are open to love

119 may

your every day
be one of sharing
love

120 *some people*
dislike me
this does not change
my love
for them

121 a cocktail
and love
will awaken
the senses

122 the wizard of love is indeed a fine friend to have

123 if you give all
that you have
with love
you will still have
everything

124 *the worship of money*
will destroy the heart and soul of love

125 all the magic of life
is in the smile
touch
and hug
of love

126 *oh dear lord*
of love
i do honor you
and your existence
and embrace

127 *even the common crow knows the true meaning of love*

KIRSTEN 大　　　　　　　　　　　DAHENSAI 正

128 the sermon of love
within a stone
cannot be heard
except
by the love
within your heart

129 *last life*
this life
all lives
i knew you
in my heart and soul
of love

130 *the embrace of peace*
love
and compassion
is lost
in the realm
of hate

131 even
in a speck of dust
love exists

132 when the mind
of trivia
knows only trivia
there is no room
for the heart
and soul of love

133 *women
in love
are the gateway
to both
heaven and earth*

all of nature
emanates love

135 the clouds
for
rain and snow
cling
to the mountain
as i cling to love
and friendship
in the merging of the souls of love

136 *poems from an unknown mystic*
speak of BIG love

love created humanity

138 *what is mind?*
it is the wind
passing through nowhere
what is love?
it is the wisdom of the gods
that teaches us love

139 my love
the importance of death
is the recycling of all humanity
and all things in existence

140 mankind
is the only creature
that poisons its own food
body
kin
and all nature and humanity
with lack of love
and compassion

141 *conception and birth*
is possible
without love
how strange

142 build a shrine
in your heart
for the veneration
of all love

143   *ah ha—*
      the path
      that most of humanity is on
      does not lead
      to love
      ha—
      i'm not on it

144   the unknown god
      of love
      is the god
      of all gods

145 it is the wisdom
of a love
that is beyond love
that is a gift of the gods

146 *love*
when you are young
love and love even more when you become old

yes
there is a love
that is beyond love
and that is my love
for you

148 never
never
underestimate
the power and energy of love

149 *courage*
my love
is the strength
to be different
from
the crowd

150 *love*
and wisdom
also come from
all
our many past lives

151 even in tears
there is a deep love

152 the first seed
of the soul
was love

153 *the beauty of flowers*
   they are no match for the love
   and beauty of the heart
   and soul of you

154 the greatest teachers
are your daily experiences
of love
in all its ways
and forms

155 *what a total bliss*
that love brings to us

156 love god
for giving you love
and life

157 all divine love
within our heart of love
is given to us
by all the gods
and all the goddesses
of divine spiritual love

158 *in the mists of time*
there always was love
and today
tomorrow
and
forever

159 into the cosmos
goes your soul seed
of love
which awaits
rebirth

160 *the holy spirit of love*
lives in all humanity
and in everything

161 only
the love in our hearts
can lead us to eternal love

162 *no one can live*
our heart of love
for us
but we can give
our love
to others

163 *a happy life*
of love
is born from the heart
of love

164 love
every part
of your body
and soul

165 *the holy spirit*
of love
exists
in every atom

166 whispers of love
and shouts of love
can come from silence and solitude

167 the source of all
is born
from the god
of all gods—
love

168 i pray
that in all my life
i will give love
to everyone and everything

169 *express your love and it will heal even strangers*

170 *the god of greed*
has no understanding
of the love
of giving
to those in need

171 the most sure sign
of love
is to do deeds
with love
and compassion

172 *when knowledge enters the heart of love*
it becomes
wisdom

173 *ecstasy*
sensuality
is the awakening
of all love
that lives in the heart
of love

174 just to talk
and hear
from you
is a blessing of love
received
in my heart of love

175 even a stone
can understand the blessing of love
and also emanate love
to those who understand it

176 love
lives in the garden of delights

177 *the blossoms of love
can bloom
everywhere*

178 *every day*
of your life
bless the path
of love

179 the divine life of love
is the everyday
life
that understands
zen

180 the mind
is never
peaceful
but
the heart
is
because of the peace of love

181 love
love
love
but
do not dominate
let it be
free

182 *my dear—*
love doing nothing
for in the nothing
everything exists

KIRSTEN ✳   DAIEN SAI ✳

183 without unconditional love
love
really
is not human love

184 *my studio*
is a place
of meditation
contemplation
love and creativity
oh joy

185 dreams
of love
are always welcome

186 all true love
has no death

187 *the pain*
that people in love
suffer
when apart
is the highest understanding
of love

188 a person
without love and compassion
already lives
in hell

189 tears of love
purify the heart
mind
and soul

190 *return*
from nothingness
to be
reborn again
to enter
the heart of love

191 to give all your heart thoughts
to love
gives birth
to all the joys
of happiness
and love

192 whoever
understands the power
that
lives in the heart
of love
can understand
nothing
and yet
everything

193 every stone buddha has a smile
of love

194 the pope's scientist
connects
your dna
to divine love

195 *if*
one lives
a life of love
they cannot hate

196 love
and give love
without any return

197 nothing
that is done
in love
is labor

198 *if you love*
one buddha
you love
all buddhas

*in the dance
of love
you will find joy
and comfort*

RICHARD KIRSTEN DAIENSAI

love is a sharing heart

201 *joy is tuning in*
to all love
including
the love that is found
in humor

202 let your love
become a river
that flows everywhere
to everyone

203 slow down
and
make room
for love
life should not be a race
to nowhere

204 *express a love*
that will reach out
and touch the hearts of everyone

205 cherish
each moment of love
as life passes
faster
than you think

206 *hugs
and touching
with love is more healing
than anyone realizes*

207 let your pandora's box
release
only love

208 *no words are needed
for the merging souls
of love*

209 negative thinking
can erase
love

210 the greatest gift you can ever give is love

211 *love*
every day
of life

212 *thanks to all the gods for a life of love*

213 love your work
and your work
will reflect
your love

214 god
creates
both
the light
and dark sides
of love

215 *forget*
the past
and live
in the garden of everyday
love

216 all
the energy
of the holy spirit
lives in the sacred heart
of love

217 pass over the bridge
and discover the treasure
of love

218 *love and cherish*
knowing that all love
is one with the love
that is in all hearts of love

219 *i quietly wait for love*
as it enters my dreams

220 even just a glance
can carry love
in it

221 how much love
does it take
to thaw out
a frozen heart?

222 *i hear and feel*
the joy of love
in your singing heart

223 how wonderful
the memories
that live
in the heart
of love

224 when somebody loves you
you are never lonely

life and love
sometimes
are like a dream
within a dream

226 *respect*
and gratitude
live in the heart and soul
of love

227 my heart
and soul of love
is one
with all the deities of all religions
and all spirituality

228 even a stone saint
has a beating heart
that emanates
a healing love

229 look
at any time
into your heart
and
your heart will tell you
how
very much
i love you

230 whispers
of love
are most enduring

231 *daiensai's art and writings*
a mirror
of creative love born
from the soul
of
everlasting love

232 *live*
in the harmony
of love
in which
the hearts of love dance

233 angels
are born
from the heart
of love

234 *energy*
energy
all energy
my love
is the energy of love

235 *i was born*
from love
and to this day
i am intoxicated
with love
and by love

236 the satori understanding of love
is the fruit
of meditations
on all forms of love
through all the ages
of love

237 a kiss of love
awakens
love
body
heart
and soul

238 *venerated*
sacred stone
sings its sutra of love
in silence

may
be a total
gem

in other

areas

(great
provider,
tender
pal)

, but
with-
out that
between-
the-sheets
sizzle,
life's just
blah.

239 if you love me
kiss me ten times
then
stop counting

240 freedom comes in many forms
but the freedom that love brings
is the best of all

241 *to love the mountains*
and the sea
is to begin a journey of fulfillment
in loving all the world

242 think love
dream love
and love will be your
reality

243 *love brings peace*
and peace brings a better world

244 the eternal pathway
to perfect love
is forgiveness

245 *you*
a sacred seed of love
were out there
in the void
waiting to be born again
and again
to love
even before
the birth
of your parents

246 the only path
to love
and inner peace
is not
through the mind
but through the heart

247 *lovers*
look and howl
with love
at the full moon

248 from love
all things
are born
to love
again

249 live in the
holy spirit
of love
for
all love is healing

250 how wonderful
to have the heart
of a puppy
that has love
from everybody
and returns
that love

251 the dove
of love and peace
does not fly
everywhere

252 love—
when you realize
that
you know nothing
that is when you know everything

253 the closer the embrace
the sweeter
the kiss
of love

254 with the death of the ego
all
becomes love
peace
joy
bliss
and tranquility

255 *do*
express
the spirituality
of
the love
that is in all things

256 without
the forces of love
nothing will exist
but the destruction
of everything

257 *if*
there is a song
in your heart
and soul
let it be
one
of love

258 love god
for the beauty of the wind
that makes nature dance
and pines sing
awakening the soul of love

259 *rejoice*
in the spirit of love
for it heals
heart
body
and soul

260 *look*
the stones
are kissing
each other
with love

261 art
love
and flowers
bring beauty into life

262 *the one smiling*
with love
is the happy one
filled
with the peace
of love

263 how short
a life of love
without devotion

264 *this life*
next life
all lives
i am crazy
crazy
with love
for you
and a life of love
in all
ways

265 *let us make*
offerings of incense
and flowers
to all the gods
and goddesses
of love
a daily ritual
of love
and gratitude

266 the ecstasy
of physical love
is relived
in the dreams of both young and old

267 sing
a song of love
to both
the rising sun
and falling petals

let us celebrate
that we
both
found love together
what a joy
love
is

269 what laid the first egg
of love?

270 *let your life
be a festival
of love*

271 *live love*
by giving love
in all ways
to those
in need
of the comfort
of love

272 free yourself
of despondency
let the heart of love
free you
and heal you

273 *sing out your love*
   and all the closed doors will open

274 hug a tree
and feel
its love of the earth

275 the soul of love
is a wanderer
that chooses
where it will be reborn

276 *old people's love*
could it not be the best love of all?

277 let us give prayers
of love and peace
to all children
of the world

278 your life
and your love
live
in
your every heartbeat

279 *love is contagious
it awakens love in others
in need of love*

280 *without*
your thoughts
and emotions
of love
love
doesn't exist within you

281 hearts
birds
flowers
bones
and stone
all speak of love
to each other

282 my love
the quicksand
of time
swallows
both
dream
and
reality

283 *in the greed*
for the fruit
one misses the flowers
and
the soul
of love

284 dear love
let us become
the ecstasy
of the stream
as it enters
the sea

285 *many
are religious
but only a few
live
the life of spiritual love*

286 love
is always
the goal
of
the lonely

287 *if you look for love*
with love
you will find love
in everything

288 *the light of love casts no shadows*

289 give love to all
and let the magic of love enter your being

290 flood
the woes of the world
with
your prayers
of healing love

291 feel love
and express love
with
your entire being
and always
give your love freely

292 *thoughts*
of love
come from the heart of love
and open
the gate
to sacred love

293 throw away
all
negative thoughts
and let all the powers
of love
transform heart
mind
and soul

294 *love*
purifies
the heart
mind
body
and soul

295 the stones
the stones
and the bones
the bones
will never tire
of their love
for each other
in their inner universe
of
ephemeral glory

296 how beautiful
the flames
of
passionate love
and even the ashes
of
the dreams of love

297 think love
talk love
sing love
eat love
drink love
dream love
embrace love

the wisdom
of a crow
speaking of love

302 a thought of love
if i am reborn
a bug
i will search
for
love
from a lady bug

303 *dogs love*
cats love
birds love
all animals love
all nature loves
stones
too
emanate love for their birth

304 *my dear love*
poverty
by choice
is not
poverty

305 one way
or
another
love
shares
the same
pillow

306 *even*
pots and pans
have
their own love
and enlightenment (shinto)

307 if
we
meditate on love
together
we can
reach the peak of love
together

308 how nice
to be told
my love
the words
i love you

309 after
a night's
sleep in oblivion
to awaken
for another day
is god's gift of life
and love

310 love
one can never
measure
its depth
until
the time of its departure

311 *never keep love*
hidden
or unspoken

312 love
and bliss
see
how they walk
hand in hand

KIRSTEN   DAIENSHI

a maiden
a beautiful woman of heaven
lived through the ages and loved all

314 if a gift is not given in love
it becomes a bribe

315 *each new day*
is a rebirth
cherish it
for it is a gift of love
from
all
gods

316 *only death*
can erase
the flame of love—
maybe

317 who is rich?
whosoever
rejoices
with love
their portion

318 love comes first
and then everything else follows

319 we all
are born
with the soul
of love
from the seed of love
in the sea of all eternities

320 *love*
or
no love
the kiss of death
makes
all creatures kin

321 all
that is
animate and inanimate
knows love
and
has
the heart of love
that is sacred

322 *keep in mind—*
the one you love
may not be here tomorrow
and your love will deepen

323 love all
but love nature
and you will help save our mother earth

324 *love others and you will love yourself*

325 when love comes your way
embrace it as it will be your friend
forever

326 untethered
love roams the world
to embrace all

327 *an empty life*
becomes
full
when love enters

328 *the kiss*
of the full moon
moves
not only
the tides of the sea
but also the emotions
of love

329   open your heart to love
and your life's journey
will be filled
with ecstasy
and end with peace of mind

330 *love like your cat*
love like your dog
let your love be unconditional
and full

331 *only fools ignore love*
when it comes their way
and they are empty

332 the light of love
is brighter than all the stars

333 *bask*
in the forever warmth
of love

334 if you make peace
with yourself
love will follow

335 do not forsake love
for it will carry you
far and wide

336 *be kind*
and caring
and love will find you

the energy of love
will heal
and give long life—
embrace love early on

338 *art
and poetry
are treasures of love*

339 my heart and soul sing
with love's excitement
whenever i hear your voice
or catch the scent of your perfume

340 always
you embellish every moment of sensual pleasure
now kiss me again
as we enter love's paradise
naked
together

341 *i love your body*
awake
or asleep
in dreams

342 should your heart feel empty of love's nectar
dear love
drink from mine
which is overflowing

343 *when we are apart*
my dear love
just the thought of you
makes my heart beat faster

344 there will never be
an end
to the eternity
of love

345 *love is both*
your in-breath
and your out-breath
the breath that is the gift
from god's love
for you

346 *let yourself go wild*
with love

347 love is magical
it gives color
and joy
in an otherwise mundane life

348 the apple
fell in love
with the woman who bit into it

349 in my sleep and dreams
it is you who enfolds me with the body and soul of love

350 love
cannot
live
with hate

meditating on love
you become love

352 *love every part*
of your physical
and spiritual
existence

353 even a tiny insect
knows and understands
love

354 how wonderful
my soul awakened
to take the blessed journey
of eternal love

355 *love is passionate*
in the temple of the heart
and even more
in the dreams of the old

356 dear one
your kiss of love
lights a holy lamp
in my heart
and soul

357 *wow*

the magic wonder
of love's bliss

358 taste the wine
of love's juices
enjoy the intoxication
of naked love

359 *galaxies*
of love
on the altar of creation

360 *to understand
love
is enlightenment*

361 *my dear love*
the moon and stars and I
get crazy at night
we make the night sky
a love bed

362 accomplishment
is a product
of love

363 *love is a feeling*
of being one
with god

364 I am old
how well I understand love
now

love
is expansive
and endless

Born in Chicago, and a longtime resident of Seattle, Richard Kirsten Daiensai spent the first 38 years of his life exploring art within the boundaries of the Western world, studying at the Art Institute of Chicago and the University of Washington. Since 1958—the year of his "awakening to the Eastern consciousness"—he has spent much of his life in Japan. In 1967 he was ordained through Buddha by Master Oshita Toyomichi Roshi of the Zuisenji Temple in Kamakura.

Daiensai's art and works appear in museums and collections around the world, including the Museum of Modern Art and Metropolitan Museum of Art, New York; Seattle Art Museum, Seattle; Library of Congress, Washington, DC; National Museum of Modern Art, Tokyo, Japan; and de Young Memorial Museum, San Francisco.